W9-BJM-503

INUIT

Leslie Strudwick

WEIGL PUBLISHERS INC.

Published by Weigl Publishers Inc.
350 5th Avenue, Suite 3304
New York, NY 10118-0069 USA
Web site: www.weigl.com

Library of Congress Cataloging-in-Publication Data

Strudwick, Leslie, 1970-
  The Inuit / by Leslie Strudwick.
     v. cm. -- (Indigenous peoples)
Includes index.
Contents: Where in the world? -- Stories and legends -- Out of the past -- Social structures -- Communication -- Law and order -- Celebrating cultures -- Art and design -- Dressing up -- Food and fun -- Great ideas -- At issue -- Into the future -- Fascinating facts.
  ISBN 1-59036-122-9 (lib. bdg. : alk. paper)
  1. Inuit--Juvenile literature. [1. Inuit. 2. Eskimos.] I. Title. II. Series.
  E99.E7S8375 2004

                    2003003962

Printed in the United States of America
1 2 3 4 5 6 7 8 9 0   07 06 05 04 03

Project Coordinator Heather C. Hudak
Design Terry Paulhus
Layout Katherine Phillips
Copy Editor Janice L. Redlin
Photo Research Pamela Wilton

Consultants
Karla Jessen Williamson, Executive Director for the Arctic Institute of North America
Dr. Robert G. Williamson, Professor and Senior Research Associate with the Arctic Institute of North America

C O N T E N T S

Where in the World?

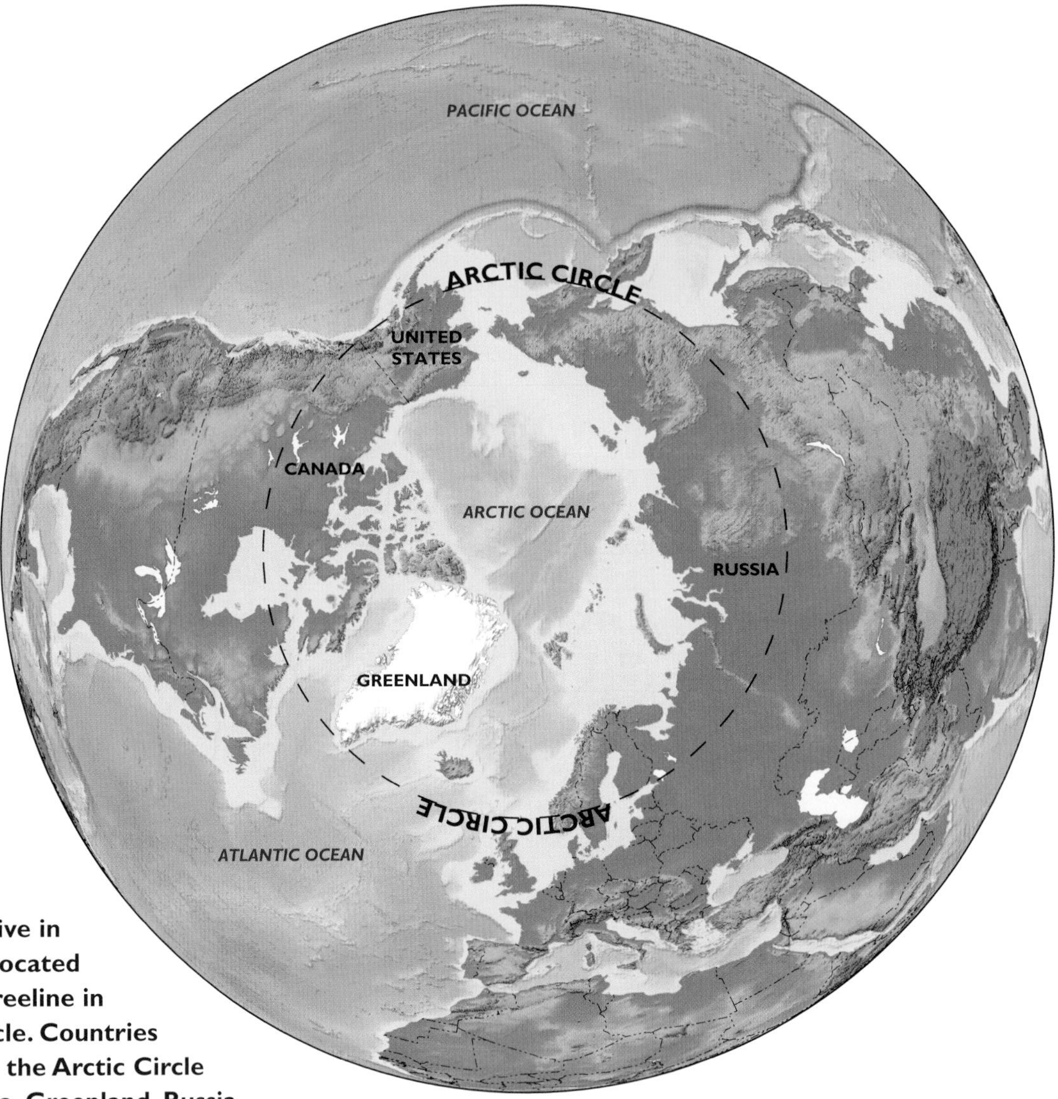

PACIFIC OCEAN

ARCTIC CIRCLE

UNITED STATES

CANADA

ARCTIC OCEAN

RUSSIA

GREENLAND

ARCTIC CIRCLE

ATLANTIC OCEAN

Inuit peoples live in communities located north of the treeline in the Arctic Circle. Countries located within the Arctic Circle include Canada, Greenland, Russia, and the United States.

The area that surrounds the North Pole where the ground stays frozen throughout the entire year is called the **Arctic**. **Inuit** live in the Arctic areas of Canada; Greenland; Russia, and the United States. Though Inuit communities are located across the Arctic landscape,

most Inuit live near water.

About 5,000 to 10,000 years ago, groups of people traveled from Asia to North America. It is believed that they crossed the Pacific Ocean using the Bering Land Bridge. Large glaciers that covered much of North America and northern Europe had not yet

melted. Sea levels were lower, exposing a large area of land. This Bering Land Bridge created a passage between Siberia and Alaska. During a hunt, **ancestors** of the Inuit followed herds of animals across the land bridge. This first group of peoples settled in the Alaska region. About

4,000 years ago, the **climate** warmed. These people, known as the Pre-Dorset culture, started to move farther east. The Pre-Dorset peoples carved tools from antlers, ivory, bone, and stone, and used **harpoons** to hunt.

The Pre-Dorset culture **evolved** over 3,000 years. They became the Dorset peoples. The Dorset lived in communities of three to fifteen families. In the summer, they lived in tents made of animal skins. In the winter, they built homes partially underground. These peoples were skilled artists. Sculptures found in the area suggest the Dorset peoples carved Arctic animals, such as birds, polar bears, and seals. The Dorset believed some of these carvings were magical.

About 1,000 years ago, early Inuit peoples from Alaska spread across the Arctic. One group, known as the Thule, traveled as far as northeastern Greenland. The Thule mainly used the bowhead whale for food and

In the Arctic, there are very few resources available to make tools and weapons. The Inuit had to be creative to make useful weapons, such as harpoons. They used walrus tusks and antlers.

tools. Their **descendants** are the Inuit of today. Modern Inuit culture evolved around 1750.

For decades, the **indigenous peoples** of the Arctic were called "Eskimos." The Ojibwa Native Peoples gave them this name, which was thought to mean "eater of raw meat." **Linguists** now believe the word Eskimo means "to net snowshoes." The word Inuit, which means "the people," was made the official name of the Arctic peoples in 1977. Inuit is the word used to describe the entire group of these indigenous peoples. One member of the group is called an Inuk.

- Husky dogs are used to pull sleds in the Arctic because they are strong and can pull heavy loads over long distances. These dogs have thick, fur coats, and they prefer living in cool climates.

- Before 1867, Alaska was part of Russia. It became part of the United States that year.

- More than 400 types of flowering plants grow in the Arctic.

- The average summer temperature in the Arctic is 50° Fahrenheit (10° C).

Stories and Legends

Creating and telling stories was an important part of Inuit culture. During the cold days and long nights of the winter months, they spent much time inside. Families and communities would make up and share stories to entertain each other. They often used songs to tell stories. The songs explained a story or described an event. Dancing was also used to tell some stories.

Inuit storytelling taught values and proper ways of doing things. It was also a way to pass Inuit history along to young people. Elders would tell stories to their children and grandchildren. Storytelling was a fun game for children. Most girls were given carved "storyknives" from their fathers. The girls used these knives to draw pictures in the ground as they told their stories. They told tales about their families, animals, and nature.

During the cold winter months, Inuit families would gather inside an igloo to stay warm and protect themselves from storms. They passed the time by sharing stories about their culture and history.

Drum dancing was an important part of most gatherings. These dances were performed to celebrate births, successful hunts, and the changing of the seasons.

Like most other cultures, the Inuit used legends to explain the creation of the world. They also told stories of spirits who watched over their peoples. For example, they believed that the **Northern Lights** were the souls of their ancestors playing kickball. They also believed that these lights were torches held by ancient ancestors to light a path for the souls of the dead.

One legend tells of the man who created the world.

He built himself wings, and a sparrow taught him how to fly. This man became a raven. With the sparrow's help, the raven created humans from clay. He also created animals for the people to hunt. To create night and day, the raven threw light and dark rocks into the sky.

Another story describes the creation of day and night. In this story, the Sun is a spirit girl who carries a torch. The Moon is her older brother. He is a good hunter. Day and night come as the boy, the Moon, chases his sister, the Sun, across the sky. The torch flickers as he tries to grab it away from his sister.

The Inuit word for the Northern Lights is *arsaniit,* which means "the kickball game."

THE STORY OF SEDNA, THE INUIT GODDESS OF THE SEA

In one version of an Inuit legend, Sedna believed she was too beautiful to marry just anyone. One day, a man wearing a dark hood offered her happiness. She agreed to marry him.

The man took Sedna to his home. It was a nest on a cliff. He took down his hood to reveal that he was a raven. He fed Sedna raw fish. Sedna was very unhappy. She called out for her father to rescue her. He arrived one year later, and they paddled away in his boat. The raven chased behind.

To lose the bird, Sedna's father tossed Sedna into the ocean. She clung to the boat, but her father hit her fingers with his paddle. Her fingers broke off and sank into the ocean. Her fingers became ocean animals.

Today, Sedna is the goddess of the sea. She sends seals and whales to the Inuit. When the Inuit have done something bad, she withholds her animals to punish them.

Out of the Past

Moravian missionaries sailed to North America in 1752, but they were not welcomed by the Inuit. Missionaries did not set sail for North America again until 1771. During this voyage, fourteen missionaries sailed to the Arctic from London, England.

Life has always been difficult for the indigenous peoples of the Arctic region. The climate has always been rugged and harsh. The Inuit, and their ancestors, have had to work hard to survive. Still, they greatly enjoy life.

Over the past 10,000 years, there have been times when the climate warmed. During these times, Inuit ancestors were able to move farther east from Alaska. Warming trends meant that more animals were available to hunt. Warm summer months allowed for a longer growing season. As a result, there were more berries to pick. When the climate cooled again, food sources were harder to find, and whole communities ended.

The Arctic climate has not changed much since the arrival of the Europeans in the 1500s. The Europeans discovered Inuit settlements while searching for a shorter

The Inuit diet included fish, seals, whales, and other sea mammals.
The flesh of these animals was cooked, dried, or frozen.

route from the Atlantic Ocean to the Pacific Ocean. Before their arrival, the Inuit did not have much contact with different cultures other than neighboring Native cultures. The arrival of the Europeans changed their lives. Many of the items the Europeans brought to the Arctic were useful. The Inuit traded furs and oil for food, guns, and supplies. Guns made hunting easier, but they also caused some changes to Inuit culture.

As a result of European settlement in the Arctic, the Inuit spent more time trapping furs to trade, which meant they spent more time hunting and less time finding food. Fewer Inuit were living the traditional **nomadic** lifestyle. Governments arrived in the North and built settlements near trading posts. These settlements included houses, nursing stations, and schools. Soon, many Inuit traded for the items they needed for their daily lives.

Along with fur traders came missionaries. Missionaries are people who spread their religion to other cultures. Sometimes, they believe they are creating a better living situation for these cultures. Although the missionaries believed they were helping the Inuit, they were actually changing the way the Inuit lived. The Inuit's traditional **spiritual** beliefs started to fade as they learned more about European culture.

TIME LINE

10,000 years ago A group of people travel from Asia to North America across the Bering Land Bridge.

5,000 years ago The Pre-Dorset peoples move east from the Bering Land Bridge, building communities in the Arctic regions.

1500s European explorers have their first encounter with Inuit communities.

1610 While searching for the Northwest Passage, Henry Hudson reaches the mouth of the Hudson River.

Early 1700s Whaling begins in the Arctic.

1771 The first missionaries arrive in the Canadian Arctic. They settle in Nain and form a mission station.

Late 1800s **Commercial** whaling stops. **Overharvesting** of whales has left too few whales in Arctic waters.

1903 The first Royal Canadian Mounted Police posts are established to maintain law and order throughout the North.

April 1, 1999 Nunavut becomes the third Canadian territory. The territory is dedicated to **preserving** the Inuit culture.

Social Structures

Family has always been very important to the Inuit. Groups of hunting families lived and worked together to increase their chances of finding and sharing food. Each person's role was equally important. In Inuit society, the roles of men and women were strictly defined. The men fished, hunted, and built houses. The women worked animal skins and dried meat after a hunt. Women also cooked and sewed clothing. Children were always expected to help. Boys helped at home until they could hunt, and girls worked with their mothers.

Inuit groups moved from place to place throughout the year. The group camped for a few months in places where

Family is the center of Inuit culture. Children learn about Inuit culture and history from the senior members of their families.

there were many animals to hunt. Each group was much like one big family. They functioned without government, tribes, and chiefs. Although some people acted as leaders, they did not tell other group members what to do. Instead, they listened to people and offered advice. These leaders were often the oldest members of the group. For example, this could be a grandmother or someone who was an experienced hunter.

A spiritual leader, or shaman, was part of most communities. The shaman was an advisor and doctor. The shaman was also able to talk to spirits. The shaman could be either a man or a woman. It was believed that people were born with the gift to see spirits and visions. A shaman was one who improved these gifts through years of training. To heal or help answer questions, the

The senior members of Inuit families ensure that special skills, such as fire making, are passed on to younger generations.

shaman spent long periods of time away from the community, and performed rituals that involved singing, dancing, and drumming.

Families in a community shared everything. When a large animal was killed, the food was divided so every family had a portion. Today, many Inuit families do not hunt for survival. Still, family is still an important part of the Inuit culture. For example, grandparents help raise the children.

THE TWO SEASONS

During the summer months, the Sun never sets in the Arctic. The land is covered with many flowering plants. During the winter months, the Sun does not rise for many weeks, or even months, depending on the region. The winter climate is bitterly cold, with heavy snowfalls and harsh winds.

Communication

Oral, or spoken, language was the most important form of communication for the Inuit. They have always used the spoken word to teach their culture and traditions to younger members of the community. Writing is a fairly new form of communication for the Inuit. Before missionaries arrived in the Arctic, the Inuit did not have a written language. There was no need to write. Living in such small groups, it was easy to share stories using just the spoken word. Children learned everything they needed to know from their parents and other adults. Ideas of right and wrong were taught through oral stories.

The Inuit began writing Inuktitut about 100 years ago. Missionaries created a writing system using the Inuit language, Inuktitut. The Inuit used this writing system, called "syllabics," to record traditions and beliefs. In some Arctic regions, the English, or Roman, alphabet is used.

There are different **dialects** of Inuktitut, but each is a variation of the same language. While some senior Inuit peoples may only speak Inuktitut, most of their children speak English as well. Some children only speak English, but many Inuit communities work to preserve their language by teaching it in school.

As other cultures introduced new objects to the Inuit, they created Inuktitut words for these items. For

The Inuit built tall, stone markers called *Inukshuk* to help guide them across the tundra. The Inukshuk were also used to guide **caribou** during hunting. Inukshuk means "like a person."

example, before European whalers arrived in the North, the Inuit did not have tea or sugar. They created the word *tii* for "tea," and *sukaq* for "sugar." More words were created when fur traders settled in the Arctic and the Inuit were introduced to spoons, kettles, and many other items.

Some other cultures believe that the Inuit have 100 different ways to say the word "snow." This is not true. There is one Inuktitut word for snow: *aput*. Similar to the English language, there are many Inuktitut words to describe different types of snow. For example, "fluffy," "slush," and "sticky" are some of the words to describe snow.

INUKTITUT

When a writing system was first introduced to the Inuit more than 100 years ago, words were spelled the way they sounded. This caused the same word to be spelled many different ways. For example, people of European descent are both *qallunaaq* and *kabloona*. Although both words are spelled differently, they are pronounced almost the same way.

Since the mid-1970s, the Inuit have tried to **standardize** the language.

Drum dancing is the most popular form of traditional Inuit music. It is still performed at gatherings and celebrations.

Law and Order

Traditional Inuit societies followed formal laws. The Inuit knew that the best way to stay alive was to always act in the best interest of the group. This helped to keep peace. The Inuit believed spirits would judge a person's behavior and punish any wrongdoing. They thought that everything had a soul. If the soul was mistreated, its spirit would return from the dead to get revenge.

Rather than written laws, the Inuit had specific rules, or principles. Since the Inuit believed animals had souls, they had respect for the animals they hunted. They treated animals with care even after the kill. They refused to hunt land and sea animals using the same weapons. If an animal was killed on land, it was cooked on land. To prevent upsetting caribou

Traditionally, the Inuit have very strict rules for hunting that have been preserved for future generations. These rules ensure that all animals are treated with respect.

spirits, it was forbidden for dogs to eat their bones on the site where the animal was killed. Since both wolves and bears were dangerous to hunt, special offerings were made to their spirits after a kill. The Inuit feared that the spirits might punish them with starvation if they did not treat the animals well.

All members of the group obeyed hunting customs. It was believed that they would suffer nature's revenge if these customs were ignored. For example, if the customs were not followed, the group believed hunts would be unsuccessful, or stormy weather would make it hard for them to hunt.

While a few communities still follow these early customs, most Inuit follow different rules today. They follow the laws of the country in which they live. However, some countries recognize Inuit laws may be more suitable than modern laws. Punishment in some Inuit communities may be different than those in large, modern cities. For example, three boys in a Canadian Inuit community attacked and injured a man. These boys were not jailed. Instead, they were **banished** to an island where no other people lived. They had to find a way to live—much like their ancestors did when they first settled in the Arctic. This was hard for the boys since they were raised in communities that had fridges, stoves, television, and other modern items.

Some Inuit offenders are given traditional sentences, such as banishment, instead of being sent to jail. People found guilty of a crime are taken to isolated areas where they are expected to live off the land.

Celebrating Culture

Inuit culture has many parts. It can be art, dance, or song. Inuit culture is also present in the way these indigenous peoples live. This includes their physical skills, the games they play, the foods they eat, and the clothing they wear. Inuit peoples believe the Arctic animals, land, sea, and weather are also part of their culture. They use the word, *illiquusiq*, which means "ways and habits," to refer to their culture and way of life.

Since Inuit culture cannot be separated from the environment, the Inuit respect their surroundings. Animals are part of their culture, so they treat them with respect. The Inuit believe that animals are on Earth to provide food and clothing for their survival. To show their respect, the Inuit only hunt as many animals as they need. All parts of an animal are used, so its life is not wasted.

Over the past 100 years, Inuit culture has changed, but many of the cultural beliefs remain the same. Although they live in houses and shop in stores for food, many Inuit still take part in hunting trips.

Family ties are an important part of Inuit culture. Inuit elders preserve their culture by passing history on to younger generations.

They build igloos to live in while they are on the hunt. The Inuit now use rifles as well as harpoons for hunting animals. Still, they continue to respect the animals that they hunt for food. They celebrate family as the core of Inuit culture. Like their ancestors, they tell stories to teach a lesson, sing to tell of a great adventure, dance to celebrate a successful hunt, and play games to bring their communities together.

Today, Inuit children have modern toys and use computers. However, they also learn about their culture and sometimes wear traditional clothes.

Art and Culture

Inuit sculptures are well-known in many parts of the world. Sculpting skills were first developed thousands of years ago when the Inuit made tools and weapons from antlers, bones, or walrus tusks. In addition to tools, they made toys and small figures for children. At first, they carved practical objects for their own families, such as combs and needle cases. Once the Europeans arrived, the Inuit traded these objects for other items.

Inuit sculptures were brought to other cultures after a young, Canadian art student named James Houston visited the Arctic in 1948. He brought some Inuit carvings to Canadian museums and stores. Houston asked the Inuit to make more carvings in return for flour, pots, and tobacco. Soon, people around the world wanted to buy these beautiful works of art. Some Inuit artists were able to earn a living creating works from antlers, bone, ivory, and stone.

Inuit peoples used clothing to display their art. Inuit women often decorated their clothing with colored fur and feathers to make different patterns. They sewed small

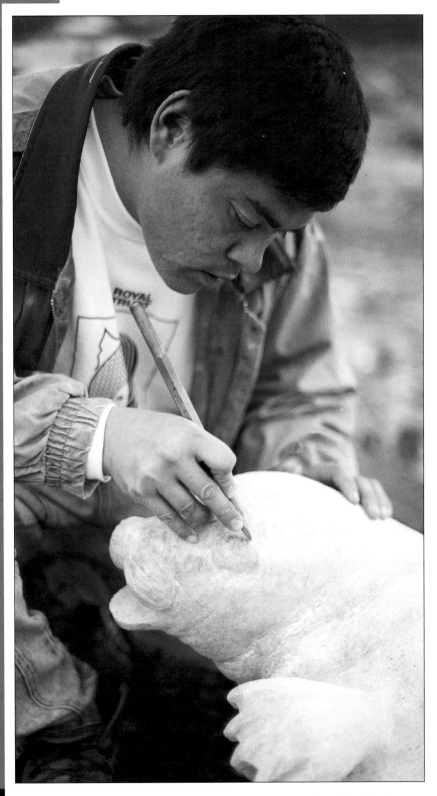

Many Inuit artists make their living by creating and selling Inuit art. Seals are a popular subject for artists.

Drawing and painting are modern types of Inuit art. Artists often draw creatures and people from traditional stories and legends.

pieces of bone, ivory, or shells to form shapes on clothes. They also used some of these items to make jewelry. Today, Inuit art is displayed and sold in many countries around the world.

More recently, Inuit artists have started to draw prints and paint. They carve images of animals, people, spirits, and mythological figures into stone. These images are covered in paint and pressed onto paper. The Inuit also paint on **canvas**. They often used their artwork to show their respect for animals and nature. Today, some villages earn their entire income by selling Inuit art.

CARVING IN STONE

Inuit artwork is most often carved in stone. Soapstone was once the most common stone used for Inuit art. Soapstone is soft and easy to carve, but it is sturdy. Today, many Inuit carve their art in a stone called serpentine. Serpentine is similar to soapstone, but it breaks less easily. Most stone is collected from a quarry near an artist's community. Often, it is possible to determine which community produced a piece of art based on the type of stone that was used.

Dressing Up

Clothes made from heavy furs and animal skin kept Inuit peoples warm. Today, the Inuit do not wear these clothes as often.

The Inuit could not have lived in the Arctic without proper clothing. They needed warm, waterproof clothing to keep warm in the chilly and windy Arctic climate.

Women made clothes from animal skins and furs. Some clothing items were made from caribou **hide**. They also used bird feathers, or fox, polar bear, and wolf furs, to make warm clothing.

Inuit usually wore a long, heavy fur coat called a parka. They also wore boots, mittens, and pants. On very cold days, they wore two layers of clothing. Body heat became trapped in the air between the layers, keeping the wearer warmer. During the summer months, lightweight, waterproof clothes were made from sealskin. From head to toe, a winter outfit could weigh as much as 10 pounds (4.5 kg).

While women's and men's clothes were very similar, there were a few differences. Women in Greenland wore thigh-high boots, which were lined with moss or dried grass. Men wore shorter boots. Women often wore parkas that had a fur-lined pouch called an *amautik*.

They used this pouch to carry their babies on their back.

Women worked hard to make clothes for their family. An animal hide was stretched and dried before it was scraped clean. To soften the hide, women chewed it with their front teeth. Chewing also helped to waterproof the hide. They sewed the seams tightly to keep out wind and cold weather. **Narwhal** or beluga whale **sinews** were often used as thread.

Although some clothing items are still made using traditional methods, most Inuit peoples buy their clothes from stores. Furs and hides are still worn to keep hunters warm during long trips.

Chewing skin to make it soft and waterproof was hard work. It could wear down women's teeth over time.

FEET FIRST

Most boots, or *kamiit*, were made from seal or caribou skins. Boots were an important part of the Inuit wardrobe. They prevent injuries that can be caused by exposure to the late springtime snow and cold temperatures.

In order to keep their feet from freezing during harsh winter weather, hunters wore boots made from shaved seal skin or haired caribou skin. These sealskin boots were waterproof and provided protection in wet regions. Haired seal skin or caribou hide boots were worn during cold, dry, winter weather.

Food and Fun

Seal meat is a healthy, traditional Inuit food. It contains many vitamins, as well as protein and iron.

As with most activities in the Arctic, it was hard to find food. The weather was too cold to grow crops, so the Inuit hunted animals as their main source of food. Being skilled hunters has kept the Inuit culture alive for thousands of years. Depending on the time of year, the Inuit hunted different animals. When the ice melted in the summer months, they hunted birds, fish, seals, walruses, and whales. During the warmer months, they also picked berries and dug plant roots from the ground. In the colder months, the Inuit hunted caribou, seals, and sometimes polar bears. The Inuit called these traditional food sources "country food."

The Inuit peoples often ate raw meat. Raw

DRIED MEAT RECIPE

- With an adult, cut meat into thin slices.
- Hang the meat over a pole outside so the pieces do not touch.
- Burn a fire beneath the meat to keep flies away.
- Turn the meat daily until dried.

food did not take much time to prepare. Raw meat also had more vitamins than cooked meat, and it was healthier for their diet. Since fruits and vegetables did not grow in the Arctic, the Inuit ate raw meat to get the vitamins they needed to stay healthy. They would dry some of the fish they caught in the summer, so it could be eaten during the winter months. Sometimes meat was cut into small pieces and dipped in salt.

To the Inuit, preparing meals and eating with friends and family was a fun activity. They thought food tasted better when it was shared, so communities ate together.

Laughing and playing was a welcome change from hunting and working. Many Inuit children and adults played games, such as sky tossing, which was the first form of trampoline. To play, one person stood in the center of a large, circular piece of animal hide. Many other people stood around the hide, holding the edges. As they pulled the edges, the person standing in the center of the hide was tossed into the air. Other games, such as arm pulling, kickball or *aqsaq*, high kicks, seal-hop, and tag required the players to use their hunting skills. Many of these games did not need equipment. Instead, they required strength and **agility**.

Inuit games, such as sky tossing, allow the whole community to have fun together.

Great Ideas

There are not many building materials in the Arctic. Since trees were not available to produce lumber, the Inuit used snow to build their houses. Many cultures call these houses igloos, but the Inuit call them *igluigaq*, which means "snow house." *Iglu* is the Inuktitut word for "house."

To build an igloo, the Inuit would cut, or saw, large blocks of packed snow. They piled these blocks on top of one another in the shape of a spiral. This formed a **dome**. They filled the cracks

Inuit peoples no longer live in igloos. Still, igloos are still used as shelter for hunters and travelers in the far North, where there are no trees to build tents.

between the blocks with snow. A low, short tunnel was built on one side of the dome. This tunnel was used as a doorway. The tunnel kept cold air from blowing into the dome. Often, a cold trap, or sunken area, was cut inside the tunnel. Inside, the igloo was covered with branches and warm furs. Igloos were usually used as temporary homes during winter hunting trips. Summer homes were built from sod or grass. Tents were built using **driftwood** and whalebones as poles and seal or caribou skins as coverings.

Dog sleds and **kayaks** helped the Inuit travel far distances for hunting. Walking was especially slow in the winter when people had to trek through deep snow wearing heavy clothing. A team of dogs could pull a sled loaded with supplies, meat, and even a few people.

Kayaks were built to fit a single rider. Made from a wooden frame and covered with sealskin, a kayak could move easily through water. It was important for kayaks to move quickly and turn easily when the Inuit were hunting large fish and whales. Several hunters would work together to catch a whale. On hunting trips, they used larger boats called *umiaks* to carry children, women, and supplies.

THE HUNTING BOAT

The Inuit used kayaks to glide through the water and hunt sea mammals. A kayak looked like a narrow canoe with a deck where harpoons could be stored. It had a wood frame that came to a point at both ends. It was covered with seal or caribou skin. The hunter sat in a small opening in the deck of the kayak. The paddler wore a special jacket made of seal **intestine**. This jacket was fitted around the edge of the opening to create a waterproof seal. To move the boat through the water, the paddler used a long paddle with a blade at each end, or a short paddle with a blade on one end. If the kayak tipped, the paddler could use the paddle to right the boat and continue the hunt.

At Issue

Many ancient Inuit customs are starting to disappear. Most Inuit peoples no longer move from one place to another in search of food. Instead, they live in settled communities. Like many modern societies, they shop at grocery stores, buy clothes, and watch television.

Though many Inuit peoples no longer hunt full-time, they still follow some of the ancient hunting traditions. However, pollution from southern regions has poisoned some of the Inuit's hunting grounds and harmed many animals. Some fish and whales may not be safe to eat.

While the Inuit have killed seals for hundreds of years and used their skins to make clothes and food, some modern cultures do not believe animals should be killed for their fur. The Inuit once ate seal meat and sold extra skins for money. Many Inuit groups depended on the money they earned trading furs and skins. Now, few other cultures will buy animal skins. Many Inuit communities have stopped practicing their ancient traditions. They no longer trade for food and other items. Instead, they use money to buy items such as blue jeans and T-shirts, canned foods, televisions, and electricity.

Self-government is another topic at issue for Inuit peoples. Before the

Caribou fur is the warmest fur available in the Arctic. It is still used to make winter clothing.

Arctic regions became part of the United States, Canada, Greenland, and Russia, the Inuit lived by their own rules. However, other countries have claimed these regions, and the Inuit are expected to obey the national laws of these countries. These laws do not always work well for Inuit communities. The Inuit would rather have their own laws and government tailored to their unique way of life.

In 1999, a new territory was created in Canada. This territory is named Nunavut, which means "our land" in Inuktitut. Most of the people living in Nunavut are Inuit. In Nunavut, Inuit work in the government to preserve Inuit traditions and create a governing system that suits the needs of these indigenous peoples. Inuktitut is the official language of Nunavut. However, **interpreters** translate in seven languages for the 26 members of Nunavut's legislature. English and Inuktitut are the most commonly used languages.

INUIT CIRCUMPOLAR CONFERENCE

In June 1977, the Inuit Circumpolar Conference (ICC) was formed to protect the interests of indigenous Arctic peoples. Inuit representatives from Alaska, Canada, and Greenland gathered in Barrow, Alaska, to determine how they could protect the culture, rights, and traditions of the Arctic peoples.

The ICC General Assembly is held every 4 years. Inuit from the Arctic regions, including Russia, gather to elect a president and **council**. During this meeting, they discuss issues regarding their rights and culture. They also establish ways to maintain Inuit culture and identity.

Since the ICC was formed in 1977, various groups have met to discuss the interests of Inuit peoples. In 1999, the Legislative Assembly of Nunavut met for the first time.

Into the Future

Today, many Inuit peoples work in modern stores and offices.

Most Inuit communities have a village or hamlet council that makes laws for the village. Since there are very few jobs in the Arctic, people must still work together as a community to survive. The local council manages community **finances.** In each community, a cooperative board of directors operates stores and exports art work, fish, furs, handmade crafts, and pelts.

Stores in Inuit villages bring modern goods and products to people. Many people want the items they see advertised on television. These communities are also connected to the rest of the world. Airplanes, boats, buses, cars, the Internet, and roads all serve to connect people living in the Arctic to other cultures. While some Inuit may still prefer to live following the traditions

of their ancestors, it is not always an option. Some of the animals they once hunted for food are now **endangered,** and it is illegal to kill them. Chemicals spilled in Arctic waters have poisoned other animals.

Inuit children no longer help their mothers sew or prepare food and skins, nor do they help their fathers hunt every day. Instead, they go to school. Arctic schools teach Inuit children about their history and traditions. Children learn traditional stories and are taught to speak Inuktitut. Students learn traditional skills such as building wooden sleds and sewing skins. They also learn about Inuit art and culture.

Some Inuit peoples have become famous outside of their communities. Susan Aglukark is a popular singer in Canada and Alaska. She sings in both English and Inuktitut. Songs such as *O Siem* and *Hina Na Ho* tell stories about the culture and concerns of the Inuit peoples.

O Siem is an expression of joy used by Inuit peoples to greet friends and family. *Hina Na Ho* is a song about surviving a cold, Arctic winter.

Kenojuak Ashevak is a well-known Inuit artist. She paints, does beadwork, draws, and carves. Born in 1927, Ashevak lived a traditional nomadic Inuit life. In 1963, the National Film Board of Canada made a film about her to document Inuit art. Although her work is sold in stores around the world, she continues to live in her Inuit community. Ashevak is a member of the Order of Canada.

Susan Aglukark released her first CD, *Arctic Rose*, in 1992 .

ATANARJUAT

In 2001, a film titled *Atanarjuat*, or *The Fast Runner*, was released. *Antanarjuat* was the first film that was written, directed, produced, and acted by Inuit.

Directed by Zacharias Kunuk, *Atanarjuat* is based on an ancient Inuit legend about a small, nomadic camp named Igloolik. An evil curse has been placed on the area of Igloolik and its peoples. The tale follows a young man named Atanarjuat as he falls in love with a woman named Atuat. However, Atuat is promised to Oki, the chief's son. Atuat marries Atanarjuart, which makes Oki very angry. Oki seeks revenge on Atanarjuat, forcing the fast runner to flee Igloolik.

This film offers a realistic look at the ancient traditions and storytelling techniques of the Inuit peoples.

Fascinating Facts

- In some areas of the Arctic, the Sun sets at the end of October and does not rise again until early February.

- When the sea ice starts to melt in summer, sharp needles of ice cover the ground. Inuit hunters put small oilskin boots on their dog's paws to prevent them from being cut by the ice.

- Inuit women once used dried sinews to sew clothing. Now, some use dental floss.

- Throat singing is a traditional form of Inuit music. Two singers stand face-to-face and repeat different sounds in fast rhythms. These sounds are similar to the sounds made by animals and birds.

- Nunavut became a Canadian territory on April 1, 1999.

- Before electricity, the Inuit burned blubber, or whale fat, in lamps to make heat and light.

- Europeans first met the Inuit in AD 984. The Vikings, led by Erik the Red, landed in Greenland and realized that Inuit were living there.

- The Inuit helped the first explorers travel to the North Pole. Admiral Robert Peary and Matthew Henson reached the North Pole on April 6, 1909.

- An Inuit village called Grise Fjord is only 500 miles (805 km) from the North Pole.

- One large whale could feed fifteen families for one year.

FURTHER READING

Waterman, Jonathan. *Arctic Crossing: A Journey Through the Northwest Passage and Inuit Culture*. New York: Knopf, 2001.

Gray-Kanatiiosh, Barbara A., and David Kanietakeron Fadden (illustrator). *Inuit*. New York: Checkerboard Library, 2002.

WEB SITES

Canada's National Inuit Organization www.tapirisat.ca

Inuit Circumpolar Conference www.inuit.org

Glossary

agility the ability to move quickly

ancestors people, plants, animals, and objects from past generations

Arctic large area surrounding the North Pole, where trees do not grow and the ground never fully thaws; the most northern part of the world

banished sent away from a community; forbidden to return to a community

canvas a strong fabric

caribou a member of the deer family with large horns

climate the weather found in a particular area

commercial to do with business or making money

council a group of people chosen to make decisions for a community

descendants people who are related to people who live after them

dialects forms of a language spoken in a specific region

dome a rounded roof

driftwood wood that is floating in a body of water or washed on a shore

endangered at risk of disappearing completely

evolved developed gradually

finances to provide money; how money is managed

harpoons spear-like weapons

hide strong, thick animal skin that is used to make leather

indigenous peoples the first settlers in a particular region or country

interpreters people whose job it is to explain what someone is saying in another language

intestine a long tube inside the body through which food travels as it is being digested

Inuit a group of indigenous peoples who live in the cold northern regions of Asia, Europe, and North America

kayaks light, narrow boats with coverings over the top

linguists people who know a language very well and study that language

narwhal sinews cords that connect the muscle and bone in a small arctic whale

nomadic regularly moving from one area to another; never settling in one place

Northern Lights bright colored beams of light that appear in the sky at night

overharvesting gathering more than is available

preserving keeping something safe or protecting something

spiritual made of, or having to do with the spirit; not of the physical world

standardize to make things of the same type have the same basic features

Index

Photograph Credits

Every reasonable effort has been made to trace ownership and to obtain permission to reprint copyright material. The publishers would be pleased to have any errors or omissions brought to their attention so that they may be corrected in subsequent printings.

Cover: Inuit boy (Lyn Hancock); **B & C Alexander:** page 6; **Corel Corporation:** pages 3, 5, 7B, 10, 11B, 12, 15, 21B, 22T, 28, 30; **M.H. Cousineau/Iglooik Isuma Productions:** page 29B; **EMI Canada:** page 29T; **Lyn Hancock:** pages 1, 7T, 11T, 13T, 13B, 14, 16, 17, 18, 19B, 19T, 20, 21T, 22B, 23, 24, 25, 26, 27; **National Archives of Canada:** pages 8 (C-124432), 9.